Mary McLeod Bethune

Sandra Donovan

Raintree

Chicago, Illinois

JB BETHUNE

© 2003 Raintree
Published by Raintree, a division of Reed Elsevier, Inc.
Chicago, Illinois
Customer Service 888-363-4266
Visit our website at www.raintreelibrary.com

For information, address the publisher
Raintree, 100 N. LaSalle, Suite 1200, Chicago, IL 60602

Printed and bound in the United States at Lake Book Manufacturing, Inc.
07 06 05 04 03
10 9 8 7 6 5 4 3 2 1

Library of Congress Cataloging-in-Publication Data

Donovan, Sandra, 1967-
  Mary McLeod Bethune / Sandra Donovan.
    p. cm. -- (African American biographies)
Summary: Recounts the life of Mary McLeod Bethune, an African American educator who fought poverty and discrimination, founded a college, and worked with Franklin Delano Roosevelt to improve opportunities for blacks.
Includes bibliographical references and index.
  ISBN 0-7398-6868-3 (HC), 1-4109-0039-8 (Pbk.)
  1. Bethune, Mary McLeod, 1875-1955--Juvenile literature. 2. African Americans--Biography--Juvenile literature. 3. African American women political activists--Biography--Juvenile literature. 4. African American women educators--Biography--Juvenile literature. 5. African American women social reformers--Biography--Juvenile literature. 6. African Americans--Civil rights--History--20th century--Juvenile literature. [1. Bethune, Mary McLeod, 1875-1955. 2. Teachers. 3. African Americans--Biography. 4. Women--Biography. 5. African Americans--Civil rights--History--20th century.] I. Title. II. Series: African American biographies (Chicago, Ill.)

E185.97.B34D66 2003
370'.92--dc21

                    2002153357

Acknowledgments
The publishers would like to thank the following for permission to reproduce photographs:
pp. 4, 17, 19, 20, 24, 29, 38, 49, 58 CORBIS; pp. 6, 51, 52, 57 Bettmann/CORBIS; pp. 8, 10, 14, 22, 30, 33, 35, 36, 41, 44 Florida State Archive; p. 12 Hulton/Archive by Getty Images; p. 43 Underwood & Underwood/CORBIS; p. 46 Hulton-Deutsch Collection/CORBIS; p. 54 Library of Congress.

Cover photograph:CORBIS

Content Consultant
Audrey T. McCluskey
Black Film Center and Archive

Some words are shown in bold, **like this.** You can find out what they mean by looking in the Glossary.

Contents

Bethune worked hard to improve educational opportunities for black people. She helped found Bethune-Bookman College.

Introduction

Mary McLeod Bethune was one of the most important African-American women of her time. She was born soon after slavery was outlawed in the United States. She died in 1955, at the beginning of the **Civil Rights** Era (1950–1970). The Civil Rights Era was a time when people worked to gain personal rights and freedoms for African Americans in the United States.

In the years between slavery and the Civil Rights Era, black people in the United States were free, but they had few opportunities. Mary worked her whole life to improve this situation. She believed that education was necessary for anyone to improve their life. She was a teacher, a school founder, and an expert on African-American youth.

Mary learned the value of education at an early age. Her father, Sam McLeod, was born a slave. He became a farmer and grew cotton when slaves in the United States were freed.

Bethune gave speeches about civil rights around the country. Here she is talking to a crowd of people at Madison Square Garden in New York.

It was hard for McLeod to support his family. When he brought his cotton to the market, white people cheated him and told him he did not have very much cotton. He knew he had more cotton than they paid him for, but there was nothing he could do.

One day, he brought his daughter Mary to the market with him. Mary was ten years old. She was the first person in her family to go to school. She could read and write.

That day at the market, Mary's father weighed his cotton. The white men told him he only had 250 pounds of cotton. But Mary could read the scale. "Isn't that 480 pounds?" she asked. The white men were angry, but they paid Sam McLeod for the 480 pounds.

That day, Mary saw how important education was to her people. She knew that African Americans would never get ahead if they did not get an education.

Sam McLeod's daughter ended up graduating from three schools. She spent the rest of her life fighting for education and other rights for African Americans. She opened a school for poor African-American children. Soon, she turned it into a college. She moved to Washington, D.C., and became friends with the president. She used her wisdom and talent to change society for the better.

This late 1800s photograph shows the small cabin in Mayesville, South Carolina, where Bethune was born.

Chapter 1:
Childhood

Mary Jane McLeod was born July 10, 1875. This was only ten years after President Abraham Lincoln freed the slaves in the United States. Mary was the fifteenth of seventeen children in her family. She was the first one who was not born a slave.

Mary was born in Mayesville, South Carolina. Her father was African and Native American. Her mother, Patsy McLeod, was African. Patsy McLeod's family had been royalty in Africa. Mary said that her mother had a great philosophy of life. Philosophy is a set of ideas about how people should live. Mary's mother did not become discouraged. She believed that people could solve problems by working hard and praying.

When the Northern states won the Civil War (1861–1865), Mary's family was **emancipated.** To be emancipated means to be freed. All slaves in the United States were emancipated in 1865.

This late 1800s photoprint shows Samuel and Patsy McIntosh McLeod. They were the parents of Mary McLeod Bethune and 16 other children.

This was the year that the Union army of the Northern States won the Civil War.

After Sam and Patsy McLeod were freed, they kept farming. But now they were paid for their work. Soon they earned enough to buy five acres of farmland from Patsy's former master. By 1870, the family owned 35 acres of farmland. They built a small log cabin with a brick chimney. They called their new home The Homestead.

When Mary was born in 1875, many of her older brothers and sisters had already moved away. About six or seven of them still lived at home. When she was a child, Mary worked on the farm with these brothers and sisters. There were no schools around for African-American children.

Mary's mother and father worked seven days a week on the farm. They grew rice and cotton. Each of the children had chores to do. Some milked cows. Some helped with washing, ironing, cleaning, and cooking. Mary picked cotton in the fields. When she was nine years old, she could pick 250 pounds of cotton a day.

School Days Begin

In the 1870s, there were very few schools for African-American children. Although the slaves had been freed, they were not allowed to go to school with white children.

In the area where Mary's family lived, there were more African-American people than white people. But there were no schools for African-American children. Instead of going to school, African-American children worked on farms, like Mary and her brothers and sisters. Their parents needed their help because they did not get paid very much for the crops they grew.

When Mary was 9 years old, a visit from Emma Wilson changed her life. Mary was out in the fields picking cotton with her

African-American children stand outside of a schoolhouse for freed slaves in the South in the 1870s.

parents when Emma stopped by and told them that she had come to start a school nearby. Emma worked for the Presbyterian Church. She asked Mary to come to her school. Mary was excited to go and learn.

Mary's new school was called Trinity Presbyterian Mission School. It was five miles from Mary's house. It was held in a one-room church. Unlike schools today, all the students from elementary school through middle school gathered in the one room to learn their lessons. They were all taught by the same teacher. The teacher used a piece of painted cardboard for a blackboard. At school, Mary learned that even though she was poor, she could make a difference in the world. She dreamed of becoming a **missionary**. A missionary is a person who teaches his or her religion to others, often in another country.

School Days End

After a few years, Mary had learned all she could at her neighborhood school. She could read and write now. She graduated in 1887, when she was 11 years old. There were no other schools in the area she could attend. She had to stay home. She went back to working all day on the family farm.

Mary wanted to keep studying. Her parents also wanted her to follow her dreams. They saved enough money to send her to another school that was farther away. But then her father's mule died, and he had to buy another one to keep the farm running. He did not have the money, so he had to use the money he had saved for Mary's school. He also had to borrow some money from a bank. If he could not pay the bank back, the bank would take his farm. Now Mary could not go away to school.

It was a hard time for Mary and her family. But they did not give up hope that things would get better. Mary said she used to kneel in the fields and pray that another opportunity would come.

Bethune was a young woman in this picture taken in 1902. At the time, she had finished her own schooling and was teaching school in Florida.

Chapter 2:
Higher Education

One year later, Mary's prayer was answered. The opportunity again came from someone Mary had never met. Mary Crissman from Colorado had heard about the little church school that Mary had attended. This woman also belonged to the Presbyterian church. The woman thought the church school was a good idea. She liked that it helped children who did not have many chances to learn.

Mary Crissman wanted to help even more. She asked Emma to pick one good student. She promised to pay for this student to attend another school to continue learning. Emma knew exactly which student to choose for this honor. She chose the student who had worked the hardest at her school. That was Mary.

Mary was very excited to be picked for this honor. She packed her few belongings and set out for her new school. It was called the Scotia Seminary. The school was like a Christian high school and college for African-American girls in Concord, North Carolina.

Mary said goodbye to her family. They could not afford to come visit her. She did not know when she would see them again. It was 1888, and she was 13 years old.

On the day Mary left for school, many of her neighbors gathered to wish her well. They brought her going-away presents like hair ribbons and scarves. Mary got on the train, and as it pulled away from the station, her neighbors started singing a song called "Climbing Jacob's Ladder." They were proud because Mary was going to climb above her hard life on the farm.

Scotia Seminary

Although Mary missed her family, she was happy to be at school. She studied English, Latin, math, and science. She wrote letters to her family to tell them what she was learning. She could not visit them because it was too far away.

The Scotia Seminary was a mission school, like Mary's first school had been. This means it was part of a church. The church paid for the school. Besides language, math, and science, the students also studied the Christian religion. Mary read the Bible every day. She wanted to know all about the Bible, so she could become a **missionary.**

These African-American women are in a cooking class at school in the late 19th century—about the time that Bethune was attendting Scotia Seminary.

Mary's new teachers also taught her sewing, cooking, laundering, and cleaning. They thought all girls should know these things. But Mary was not interested in cooking and sewing. She had once heard a **missionary** give a speech about Africa and the need for teachers there. Ever since then, Mary had dreamed of being a missionary in Africa. She wanted to teach others what she had learned. She was also very religious, and she wanted to share the teachings of the Presbyterian church.

Mary spent seven years at Scotia Seminary. She went to classes all day long. After class, she worked in the school's laundry and kitchen to earn money. Twice during those seven years, she saved enough money to visit her family.

At Scotia Seminary, Mary saw white and African-American teachers working side by side. This taught her about possibilities for African-American women. She graduated in 1894, when she was 19 years old.

Moody Bible Institute

After Mary graduated from Scotia Seminary, she asked the Presbyterian church to send her to Africa as a missionary. However, they said she was not ready yet, and that she should study more. Mary liked to study, so she was not disappointed.

Dwight Moody founded the Bible Institute for Home and Foreign Missions to teach people to be missionaries.

Mary got a **scholarship** to another school. A scholarship means that someone's school fees are paid for by someone else. Mary moved north, all the way to Chicago. She went to the Bible Institute for Home and Foreign Missions in Chicago. This school prepared people to be missionaries. Mary was the only African American out of more than one thousand students.

African-American graduates of a mission school pose for a photo. Church officials would not let African Americans become missionaries because they were black.

Mary spent two years at the Bible Institute for Home and Foreign Missions. She studied more about religion and mission work. **Missionaries** do many kinds of work. Sometimes, they teach people about the Christian religion. Other times, they teach people how to read and write. In Chicago, Mary did missionary work. She worked among poor people. She helped feed the homeless. She taught them about the Bible. She visited poor people at home and in jail. She helped to start Sunday schools for poor children.

Mary graduated from this school in 1896, when she was 21 years old. By the time she graduated, the school had changed its name to the Moody Bible Institute.

Mary thought she was now ready to be a missionary. After graduation, Mary again asked the church to send her to Africa as a missionary. But the church told her they did not send African-American people to be missionaries. They only sent white people. At that time, the churches were run by white people, and many of them did not think black people were smart enough to become missionaries. They thought this even though black people went to mission schools like Mary did.

Mary was crushed. She had dreamed of being a missionary for more than ten years. She could not believe she could not become a missionary simply because she was black. She later said this was the biggest disappointment of her life.

Mary returned to Mayesville to help her father after graduating from the Moody Bible Institute in 1896.

Chapter 3:
A Teacher

Mary was sad that she could not become a **missionary**, and she returned to her family in Mayesville. She did not stay sad for long, though. She decided to make the best of her situation. One thing she wanted to do was earn some money to help her father. He needed to pay the bank that had loaned him money for his mule.

In the 1890s, there were few opportunities for African-American women. Even if they had graduated from college like Mary had, there were not many jobs available. In the South, there were even fewer opportunities. African Americans were more **segregated** in the South than in the North. Laws and actions kept them separated from white people. For instance, they could not go to the same schools. They could not stay in the same hotels. African Americans, and especially African-American women, usually could not get good jobs either.

This 1916 picture shows what a one-room African-American classroom in Kentucky looked like. Mary taught at schools like this one.

Teaching was one job open to African-American women. They could not teach white children, but they could teach African-American children. Mary thought this would be a good job because she would still be following her dream of helping people.

Mary applied for some teaching jobs as soon as she graduated. She wanted to stay in the South. She wanted to be close to her family, and she also wanted to help African-American children who had the hardest lives. These were the children in the South.

First Job

Mary's first teaching job was in Augusta, Georgia. She became a teacher at the Haines Institute. This was a mission school for African-American children. The students did not know how to read and write, and neither did their parents. They reminded Mary of herself when she first went to school.

Mary taught the children to read and write. She also taught them math and science, and taught them about the Bible. She sent money home to her family.

The principal of the Haines Institute was an African-American woman named Lucy Laney. Just like Mary, Lucy was the daughter of former slaves. Also just like Mary, Lucy thought all children should be able to go to school. Bethune learned a lot from Laney. She learned how important education is to poor people.

Mary got a new vision from Lucy Laney. A vision is an idea of what your purpose in life is. Mary's new vision was that she would do good by teaching children in her own country instead of in Africa. She was no longer sad that she could not be a **missionary**. She wanted to help more African-American children by teaching them.

Lucy Laney

Lucy Laney was born in 1854, twenty years before Mary McLeod Bethune was born. Both women worked throughout their lives to make education available to poor African-American children.

When Laney was ten years old, the Civil War ended, and slaves were freed across the United States. Although they were free, most blacks did not have the opportunity to go to school. In Macon, Georgia some freed slaves worked together with a church to start a high school for African Americans. Laney attended this school and graduated when she was 16. That same year, a college for African Americans called Atlanta University opened. Laney entered Atlanta University and graduated with the first group of graduates in 1873.

For ten years, Laney taught at African-American schools in the Georgia cities of Milledgeville, Savannah, and Augusta. Her dream was to open her own school, but she did not have the money. Then in 1883 she raised money from the community and from the Presbyterian church to open a school in Augusta. It was called the Haines Normal and Industrial School. It was named after Mrs. F.E.H. Haines, a wealthy member of the Presbyterian church who donated money.

The Haines Institute was a mission school for African-American children. Laney's school became a model for African-American schools across the South. Mary McLeod Bethune even taught there.

Mary was not pleased with a lot of schools for African-American women. She thought that the schools mostly taught these women to do hard jobs like cooking and cleaning for others. These jobs did not pay well, and they did not offer much opportunity to African-American women. Mary wanted to teach them to be leaders in their community. She wanted to make sure they knew history and math and science.

A Family

In 1897, Mary moved to South Carolina to teach at another school. There, she met a man named Albertus Bethune. She met him in church, where he sang in the choir. He was five years older than she was. He was also a teacher.

A year later, Mary and Albertus married. It was 1898, and Mary was 23 years old. Now her name became Mary McLeod Bethune. The Bethunes moved to Savannah, Georgia. They both taught school. However, Albertus did not like teaching as much as Mary did. Soon, he got a job as a porter. A porter is someone who helps carry people's bags at a train station or hotel. He earned more money as a porter than he did as a teacher.

Mary kept teaching. She liked it very much. In 1899 she gave birth to a baby boy. She named him Albert and called him Bert. After Bert was born, Bethune stopped teaching for one year. She wanted to spend as much time as she could with her baby son.

After one year, Bethune got another job as a teacher. She kept sending money home to her parents. Bethune taught at many schools in the next few years. Her husband held many different jobs in Savannah during this time. Sometimes he taught school. Other times he was a porter. He also worked as a salesman.

In Savannah, Mary met the pastor from a Presbyterian church in Palatka, Florida. He told Mary that many people needed help. There were many African American families living in Florida. But there were few schools for these children. He wanted Mary to move there and start a school in his church.

Florida

In 1900, the Bethune family moved to Palatka, Florida. Bethune opened a Presbyterian church school. She taught local children and helped people in the community. She visited jails several times a week. She started clubs for young people.

At her school, Bethune taught African-American children whose parents did not have much money. Bethune did not have much money herself. Besides teaching, she sold life insurance in order to make enough money to live.

Bethune found it hard to keep her school going in Palatka. Many families were moving away from this small town. They were moving to the east coast of Florida, along the Atlantic Ocean.

This 1937 photo shows African-American railroad workers repairing a section of track in a swamp in Osceola National Forest in Florida. Mary hoped to teach the children of these railroad workers.

At the time, a railroad company was building a railroad along this coast. This meant there were plenty of jobs for African-American men doing railroad construction. Hundreds of families moved to Daytona and other cities along the Florida coast.

Bethune soon followed. There were no church schools open in this area. She wanted to open a school for the children of these families.

This 1911 picture shows Bethune at her desk at school. Bethune was the principal of the Daytona Educational and Industrial School for Training Negro Girls.

Chapter 4:
A New School

Bethune moved to Daytona, Florida, in September of 1904. Her husband did not want her to go, but she wanted to follow her dream. Bethune found it hard to be married to Albertus and still be true to her dream of helping people. Their six-year marriage had not been happy. Bethune decided to move to Daytona without her husband. Albertus could not find work in Florida and moved back to his family's home in South Carolina. They never lived together again, but they did not divorce. Albertus died in 1919.

Bethune traveled to Daytona with her son, Bert. She had $1.50 in her pocket. She stayed at a friend's house for a while. She was determined to open a school soon.

Bethune spent her days looking for a building for her new school. She walked all over the city, and told people that she wanted to open a school. Many people thought she was crazy.

They said she did not have enough money to open a school. They also said that poor children needed to work to help support their families. They did not have time to go to school.

Bethune finally found a run-down cottage. It had four rooms, and it needed a lot of work. The rent was $11 a month. Bethune gave the owner her $1.50 and promised to have the rest by the end of the month.

Bethune had only a few weeks to earn the $9.50 she needed for rent. She asked everybody she met for money. Somehow she scraped together enough money to pay the first month's rent. She and Bert moved into two of the rooms, and she used the others for her classrooms.

School Opens

On October 3, 1904, Bethune's little school opened. She named it the Daytona Educational and Industrial School for Negro Girls. She had six students. There were five girls and Bert, who was 4 years old. The girls were between the ages of 8 and 12. Their parents paid Bethune 50 cents a week for **tuition.** This was their fee for attending school. It was all the money Bethune had to run her school, but it did not cover many of her costs.

Bethune knew how to run a school without much money. She used old boxes for desks. She burned logs and used the charred

Mary McLeod Bethune leads a line of girls from the Daytona Educational and Industrial School for Negro Girls school in 1904.

splinters for pencils. She crushed berries and used the juice for ink. The school was next to the city's garbage dump. Bethune hunted through the dump for things she could use. She found all kinds of things other people did not want any more. She found broken chairs and other pieces of furniture. She found cracked dishes and old pots. She showed her students how to wash and fix everything. This was part of their education. They were learning how to improve their lives.

Many of Bethune's students had to walk a long way to school. Soon they started sleeping overnight at the school. Bethune had to find a place for them to sleep.

People in the area heard about what she was doing and some gave her money. Bethune used it to rent a bigger building next door to the school. She made her own mattresses with corn sacks and Spanish moss. Spanish moss is a vine that grows on trees in the South. Bethune dried the vines and stuffed them into the sacks.

School Grows

Bethune's Daytona Educational and Industrial School for Negro Girls grew quickly. Most of her students were girls. Bethune thought it was most important to teach girls. In those days, girls had fewer opportunities than boys to learn. Bethune was following her dream of teaching these girls how to improve their lives.

These students are taking care of the animals at the barn of the Daytona Educational and Industrial School for Negro Girls.

These students wear aprons for a cooking class at the Daytona Educational and Industrial School for Negro Girls, 1910 or 1911.

As Daytona Educational and Industrial School for Negro Girls grew, Bethune needed teachers. Some teachers volunteered. This meant they worked for free. Other teachers earned between $15 and $25 a month. All of the teachers could sleep and eat at the school.

Bethune planted a large garden behind the school. She taught the students how to grow vegetables. She also taught them how to cook. She wanted her students to know how to take care of themselves. The students ate the foods they grew and cooked.

Bethune and the students also earned money from the vegetable garden. They sold vegetables to local people. Bethune also made sweet potato pies, and sold them to the railroad workers.

Bethune was supposed to pay herself with any money left over. But she never had money left over. She had a place to sleep and enough to eat, but she did not have any money. She wore hand-me-down clothes. Often, the students practiced sewing on these clothes. They remade the old clothes to fit Bethune. This is where she got most of her clothes that she wore everyday.

Soon, Bethune realized that she was not making enough money to keep her school running. She knew that she was spending too much money on rent. She also knew that she needed to buy land for the school. How would she find enough money to buy land?

Bethune started Bethune-Cookman College as a way to teach African Americans the skills they needed to get good jobs. The photo above, taken in 1943, shows students learning auto mechanics at the college.

Chapter 5:
The Bethune-Cookman College

Once again, Bethune did not let being poor stand in the way of her dreams. She wanted to expand her school with a new **campus.** A campus is the land and buildings of a school. Even though she had no money, she started looking for land and buildings to buy in about 1905.

Soon she realized she would never get enough money to buy buildings for her school. She would have to build them herself. So, she began looking for land to build on. The first place she looked was right in her own backyard: the city dump.

This large field had been empty for years and people from all over Daytona brought their garbage there. The owner wanted to sell it for $250. Every day, Bethune talked to him and tried to work out a deal. Finally, the owner agreed to take $5 at first, and the rest within two years.

The only problem was that Bethune did not even have $5. But she did not tell the owner that. Instead, she told him she would be back with the money in a few days. Then, she baked a large batch of sweet potato pies. She took these to the railroad construction site and sold them to the workers. Two days later, she handed the owner a handful of coins wrapped up in a handkerchief. The coins added up to $5.

A Schoolhouse

Now that Bethune had land for her school, she needed a building for classes. She also needed a place for students to eat and sleep. However, buildings cost a lot of money.

Bethune did what she had done to open her school in the first place. She asked everybody to help her. She asked builders to give her loads of sand and concrete. She asked carpenters to help her for a few hours each evening. In return, she would make them sandwiches. She also offered to teach their children for free. She even taught many adults to read and write in the evenings.

Slowly, the building went up. It opened in 1907. Bethune named it Faith Hall because it took a lot of faith to get it built. By this time, she had about 250 students and four teachers.

Soon, Bethune's school added two years of college classes as well as the full high-school program. She offered special training in

This is what Bethune's office looked like in the 1950s at the Bethune-Cookman College in Daytona Beach, Florida.

teaching and nursing. The school outgrew Faith Hall and added another building named White Hall in 1916. Bethune renamed the school the Daytona Normal and Industrial Institute.

In 1923, her school joined with another school called the Cookman Institute. The Cookman Institute was a nearby school for boys. The new school was called the Daytona-Cookman Collegiate Institute. It was later renamed the Bethune-Cookman College in 1931. Bethune's dream had started out as a school for children, but had turned into a college for teenagers. Bethune was now making a difference in the lives of thousands of young people.

Raising Money

It took a lot of hard work to get enough money for the Bethune-Cookman **campus.** But even after it was built, Bethune still needed money to run the school. Most of her students did not have much money to pay for their education. Bethune needed to pay teachers, buy supplies, and fix up the campus. All this cost money.

Bethune continued to ask everybody for contributions. A contribution is something given by one person to another person. It can be money, objects, or time. Bethune asked people for all of these things. She asked people to give time to teach and to help her build her campus. She asked for objects like furniture. And she asked for money.

Marcus Garvey

While Mary McLeod Bethune was trying to help African Americans find a better life in the United States, another man, Marcus Garvey, was urging them to go "back to Africa." Garvey believed that blacks would never be treated fairly in countries where most of the people were white. He preached that African Americans should consider Africa their homeland and that they should go there to live.

Marcus Garvey is dressed up for a ride in an early 1920s parade.

Born in 1887, Garvey began his back-to-Africa movement in Jamaica in 1914. He brought the movement to New York City in 1916. By the early 1920s, Garvey had about 2 million followers. Most of his followers were poor African Americans, yet they sent him thousands of dollars. He used the money to set up some all-black businesses.

His plans collapsed, however, when he was sent to prison in 1925 for making some poor business decisions. When he was released from prison in 1927, he returned to his own homeland of Jamaica.

These students are marching in the 1946 graduation procession at Bethune-Cookman College.

Bethune spent a lot of her time asking people for money. She wrote long letters to important people throughout the community. She also traveled across Florida to ask for contributions. Sometimes people gave her money. Other times she came home empty-handed.

One day, Bethune arranged a meeting at a fancy hotel in Daytona. She planned to talk to a large group of wealthy people and ask them for contributions. However, when she arrived, there were only six people in the audience. Bethune was disappointed there were so few people, but she gave a long speech anyway.

She told the six people about her students. She told them that her students were poor. She explained that they needed an education, so they would have a fair chance in life. She asked everyone for any help they could give. At the end of her speech, only one man gave Bethune some money. He gave her $20.

Bethune was disappointed that she only raised $20 after her long speech. But she thanked the man and returned home to her school. The next day, the same man showed up to look around the school. He saw that the **campus** needed a lot of work. He saw a broken-down sewing machine in the sewing class. In the kitchen, he saw a box of cornmeal on a shelf. He asked what else there was for the children to eat. Bethune said that was all they had.

That day, the man gave Bethune $250. The next day, he came back with a brand-new sewing machine. It turned out he was Mr. Thomas H. White, the owner of a sewing machine company. Soon, he was bringing clothes and food and other things needed at the school. He became one of the school's biggest contributors. When he died, he left $67,000 to the Bethune-Cookman College.

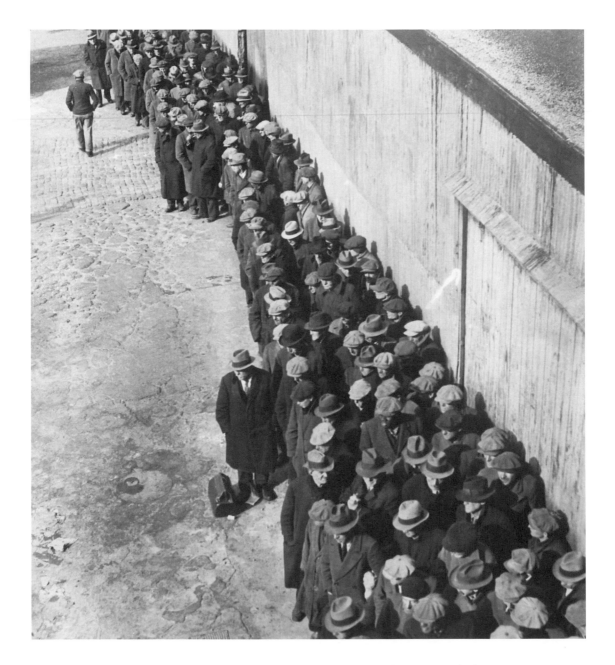

The Great Depression affected all parts of the country. Above, people line up for soup in New York in 1935.

Chapter 6:
Fighting for Fairness

In 1929, the stock market crash brought big changes to the United States. Before then, many people had plenty of money. They bought stocks, which are small pieces of ownership in companies. But the companies failed, and the stocks were soon worthless. Banks closed, and millions of people lost their life savings. People everywhere lost their jobs and their homes. And African Americans in the South, who had been poor before, suffered the most. They had little to lose in the first place. When everybody lost money, life became hardest for the poorest.

This difficult period of time was called the **Great Depression** (1929–1939). Hungry people lined up for blocks to get a bowl of free soup. African Americans had been treated badly before the Great Depression. Now that there were not enough jobs or food across the country, people treated them even worse. It seemed that African Americans would lose everything they had struggled to gain.

This made Bethune work even harder for the causes she believed in. She kept reminding people that her school needed money. People did not have much money to give anymore, but many continued to help the school. Bethune told people that now it was more important than ever to help poor people.

Friend of the President

Bethune was not the only person who cared about poor people during the **Great Depression.** Many people were worried about the lack of jobs in the country. In 1932, Americans elected Franklin Delano Roosevelt as U.S. president. Roosevelt went to work right away trying to help jobless and homeless Americans. He set up programs to give people jobs building roads and buildings. He put government money into programs to feed poor people. He called his projects the **New Deal.**

Bethune agreed with these new programs of the President. But she thought there was still a lot of **discrimination** against African Americans. Discrimination is unfair treatment based on who a person is.

The government often **discriminated** against African Americans because government jobs and money usually went first to white people. If there was any left over, they went African Americans. President Roosevelt wanted to change this pattern. He asked Bethune to help him.

In 1943, Bethune (second from left) and Eleanor Roosevelt (second from right) visited George Washington Carver Hall, a dormitory for African-American men at Howard University in Washington, D.C.

Bethune worked hard to end discrimination. She gave speeches and wrote many magazine articles. She talked about the importance of education and **civil rights** for African Americans. Civil rights are the personal freedoms that are guaranteed to all U.S. citizens.

In 1935, Bethune won an award called the Spingarn Medal from the **National Association for the Advancement of Colored People (NAACP)**. The NAACP is a national group that works to gain equal rights for African Americans. After she won this award, more and more people from all over the country wanted to hear her opinions on education and **civil rights.** She became good friends with the President and his wife, Eleanor Roosevelt. They invited her to the White House and listened to her advice on civil rights.

In 1935, Bethune formed a group called the National Council of Negro Women in Washington, D.C. This group **organized** clubs across the country. In these clubs, African-American women talked about issues such as civil rights and opportunities. Being in these clubs gave African-American women more power than they usually had in society in the 1930s. Bethune was president of this council until 1949. She helped to form almost 90 local clubs across the country.

In 1936, Bethune received another great honor. President Roosevelt asked her to work for the National Youth Administration (NYA). The NYA was part of Roosevelt's **New Deal.** It helped train young people for jobs. Bethune soon became Director of Negro Affairs for the NYA. This job made her one of the most powerful women in the country. She held the highest government job that any African-American woman had ever held. She helped find part-time work for young African Americans, so they could stay in college.

Government Work

For the next ten years, Bethune lived mostly in Washington, D.C. She helped President Roosevelt with many projects. One of them

Bethune took a break from her job as main speaker at the 1937 National Conference on the Problems of the Negro and Negro Youth to talk to Eleanor Roosevelt (right).

was the Fair Employment Practices Committee. This was a government group that worked to end job discrimination in the United States.

As part of his **New Deal,** President Roosevelt had hired some African Americans for important government jobs for the first time. Even though they held these jobs, Bethune did not think African Americans had enough power in Washington. So, she **organized**

President Harry S Truman (seated) signs a bill in 1948 declaring February 1 "National Freedom Day." Bethune (center) and African-American representatives, including Black Cabinet members, look on.

weekly meetings in her apartment where these men and women could discuss ideas and projects. This group later became official and advised the president on many issues. It was called the Federal **Cabinet** on Negro Affairs, also known as the Black Cabinet. A cabinet is a group of people that give advice to a president or other leader.

Bethune became so busy with government work that she no longer had enough time to be in charge of Bethune-Cookman College. In 1942, she hired another person to be president of the college. Still, she often traveled back to Florida to check on her school.

The Right to Vote

In the 1920s, there were Jim Crow laws in the United States. These laws kept white people and black people separate. Black people were treated unfairly. Voting was one example of this. Even though it was the law, many African Americans could not really vote. Sometimes when they got to the voting booth, white people in charge sent them away. Sometimes African Americans had to prove that they could read and write before they were allowed to vote. This was against the law, but it happened often. Not all white people wanted to stop African Americans from voting, but the ones who did were very powerful. Some of them were in a group called the **Ku Klux Klan.** The Ku Klux Klan **discriminates** against people who are not white and Christian. Ku Klux Klan members threatened to kill African Americans. Many times they did kill them. This made many African Americans afraid to vote. But Mary McLeod Bethune was not afraid. Ku Klux Klan members threatened her, but she and all of the teachers at her school voted in elections every year.

This picture of Bethune was taken in 1950. Bethune began to have breathing problems when she got older. This made it harder for her to do her work.

Chapter 7:
A Meaningful Life

Bethune continued to work hard, even as she got older. But this work was hard on her health. Sometimes she thought only about taking care of other people and did not spend enough time taking care of herself. She wanted to follow her vision, and she wanted to leave the world a better place than it was when she entered it. But she was overweight and had trouble breathing. When she was 65 years old, she had to go to the hospital for an operation to help her breathe better.

In 1940, she checked into Johns Hopkins Hospital in Baltimore, Maryland, for her operation. Being in the hospital did not slow her down. She held meetings with important leaders in her hospital room. She also continued to fight for the rights of African Americans. When she realized that the hospital had no African-American doctors, she insisted that two be brought in to watch her operation. Johns Hopkins became one of the first hospitals in the country to have white and African-American doctors working together.

World War II

After her operation, Bethune's doctors ordered her to slow down. But she had become very important in Washington, D.C. During World War II (1939–1945), she helped to get African American women admitted to the Women's Army Corps (WAC). At the beginning of the war, only white women were allowed to train to become officers in the WAC. With Bethune's help, the law was changed in 1942. Bethune then became Special Assistant to the Secretary of War. She was in charge of selecting women to go to officers' training school. She used her position to protest the **segregation** of African Americans in the U.S. armed forces.

Bethune put all of her energy into the war effort. She did not like that soldiers were **segregated,** but she worked to make sure that all soldiers were treated well. She raised money for wounded soldiers and helped collect blood for hospitals. She also wrote letters to many soldiers on the battlefields.

After the war, President Roosevelt created a plan for a worldwide group to promote peace. This group became the United Nations. Roosevelt asked Bethune to attend the **organizing** meeting for the United Nations. Out of 50 people attending, Bethune was the only African American.

The Retreat

By 1950, when Bethune was 75 years old, she was not strong enough to keep up her busy schedule in Washington. She returned

Bethune giving advice to members of the women's Auxiliary Army Corps in Fort Des Moines, Iowa, in 1942. She helped pick black women to be officers.

to her home on the Bethune-Cookman **campus.** She called this home The Retreat. At The Retreat she continued to write about **civil rights.** Many people still asked for her advice. President Harry S Truman asked her to be on the Committee for National Defense. He also asked her to go to Liberia, in Africa, to represent the United States at the second **inauguration** of President William V.S. Tubman. An inauguration is an official ceremony when a new president begins a term. In 1953, at the age of 78, Bethune finally made it to Africa to attend this inauguration.

Bethune is talking with young women outside White Hall on the Bethune-Cookman College campus in 1940.

Two years later, on May 18, 1955, Mary McLeod Bethune died from a heart attack. She was 79 years old. She was buried on the **campus** of Bethune-Cookman College. People from across the country came to her funeral to honor her legacy. A legacy is something that a person passes on to the world when he or she dies. Her legacy was giving young people the opportunity to improve their lives.

Legacy

Today, people have not forgotten Mary McLeod Bethune's legacy. Students from around the country still attend the Bethune-Cookman College. Bethune's home on the campus is now a National Historic Landmark. This means it is protected by the government because it is a piece of history. Another building in Washington, D.C., where Bethune once led the National Council of Negro Women, is now a museum of African-American women. In 1985, the U.S. Postal Service issued a 22-cent stamp honoring Bethune.

In 1974, a statue of Bethune was completed in Lincoln Park, in Washington, D.C. The statue is inscribed with her legacy, words she wrote a few years before she died:

"I leave you love. I leave you hope. I leave you the challenge of developing confidence in one another. I leave you a thirst for education. I leave you a respect for the use of power. I leave you faith. I leave you racial dignity. I leave you a desire to live harmoniously with your fellow men. I leave you, finally, a responsibility to our young people."

Glossary

cabinet   group of people who give advice to a president or other leader

campus   land and buildings of a school

civil rights   personal freedoms that are guaranteed to all U. S. citizens

discriminate   to treat a certain group of people badly because of race, religion, or gender

discrimination   act of treating someone unfairly because of appearance or other qualities a person is born with

emancipate   to free from slavery

Great Depression   years from 1929 to 1939, when millions of Americans were jobless and homeless

inauguration   official ceremony when a new president begins a term

Ku Klux Klan   group that discriminates against people who are not white and Christian

missionary   person who works for a church and tries to help poor people

National Association for the Advancement of Colored People (NAACP)   national group that works to gain equal rights for African Americans

New Deal   government programs put in place in the 1930s by President Franklin Delano Roosevelt to help poor people during the Great Depression

organize   to plan

scholarship   arrangement where someone pays for someone to go to school

segregate   to keep separate. Actions and laws in the United States often segregated African American people from white people.

segregation   rules or laws that force a group of people to live apart from each other

tuition   fee for attending a school

Timeline

1875: Mary McLeod is born in Mayesville, South Carolina.

1885: Begins school at Trinity Presbyterian Mission School near her home.

1887: Graduates from Trinity Presbyterian Mission School.

1888: Begins Scotia Seminary in Concord, North Carolina.

1894: Graduates from Scotia Seminary, begins Moody Bible Institute in Chicago.

1895: Graduated from Moody Bible Institute.

1896: Begins first teaching job in Georgia.

1898: Marries Albertus Bethune.

1899: Gives birth to a son, Albert McLeod Bethune.

1904: Opens Daytona Educational and Industrial Institute for Negro Girls.

1923: Daytona Institute joins another school and becomes Bethune-Cookman College.

1935: Receives the Spingarn medal from the National Association of Colored People.

Forms the National Council of Negro Women in Washington, D.C.

1936: Begins full-time job with National Youth Administration; later becomes Director of Negro Affairs.

1942: Women's Army Corps begins training women to be officers; Bethune helps make sure that African-American women are included.

1945: Attends the **organizing** conference for the United Nations.

1953: Makes her first visit to Africa.

1955: Dies at age 79.

Further Information

Further reading

Halasa, Malu, et al. *Mary McLeod Bethune: Educator.* Broomall, Penn.: Chelsea House, 1993.

Jones, Amy Robon. *Mary McLeod Bethune.* Chanhassen, Minn.: The Child's World, 2001.

Kelso, Richard, et al. *Building a Dream: Mary Bethune's* School. Chicago: Raintree, 1992.

Addresses

Mary McLeod Bethune Council
House National Historic Site
1318 Vermont Avenue NW
Washington, DC 20005

Bethune-Cookman College
640 Mary McLeod Bethune Blvd.
    Daytona Beach, FL 32114-3099

Mary McLeod Bethune Archives and
Photographs
Florida Department of State
Division of Library & Information
Services
Bureau of Archives & Records
Management
500 S. Bronough Street
Tallahassee, FL 32399-0250

Index